Nelson

MATH FOCUS 1

**Senior Author and Senior
Consultant**
Marian Small

Authors
Manuel Silva
Joanne Simmons
Marian Small
Bryan Szumlas
Paula Watson

Assessment Consultant
Sandra Carl Townsend

Mathematics Consultant
Shirley Barrett

THOMSON

NELSON

Australia   Canada   Mexico   Singapore   Spain   United Kingdom   United States

Nelson Math Focus 1

**Senior Author and
Senior Consultant**
Marian Small

Authors
Manuel Silva
Joanne Simmons
Marian Small
Bryan Szumlas
Paula Watson

Assessment Consultant
Sandra Carl Townsend

Mathematics Consultant
Shirley Barrett

Director of Publishing
Beverley Buxton

**General Manager, Mathematics,
Science, and Technology**
Lenore Brooks

Publisher, Mathematics
Colin Garnham

Associate Publisher, Mathematics
Sandra McTavish

Managing Editor, Development
David Spiegel

**Program Manager, First Folio
Resource Group, Inc.**
Fran Cohen

**Developmental Editors, First Folio
Resource Group, Inc.**
Susan Petersiel Berg
Brenda McLoughlin
Sasha Patton

**Art Manuscripts, First Folio
Resource Group, Inc.**
Linda Watson

Assistant Editor
Carmen Yu

Editorial Assistant
Caroline Winter

**Executive Director, Content and
Media Production**
Renate McCloy

**Director, Content and Media
Production**
Linh Vu

**Senior Content Production
Manager**
Carol Martin

Copy Editor
Shana Hayes

Production Manager
Cathy Deak

Senior Production Coordinator
Sharon Latta Paterson

Design Director
Ken Phipps

Art Management
Suzanne Peden

Design and Composition
Peggy Rhodes

Cover Design
Wil Bache
Eugene Lo

Cover Image
Jennifer Westmoreland/
ShutterStock

Printer
RR Donnelley/Willard

Table of Contents

Can You See a Pattern?

by Jill Bever and Sheilah Currie

Can you see a pattern?

Can you see a pattern?

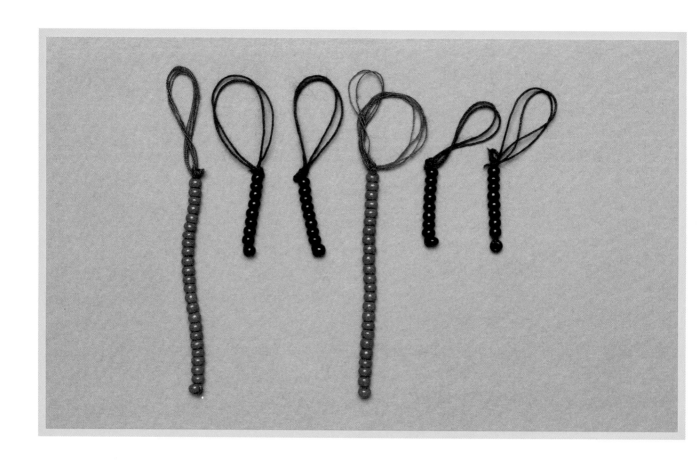

10

Act It Out

Here is Ben's pattern.

Make Ben's pattern.

Keep Ben's pattern going.
Use more beads.

Can you make a different pattern?
Try it!

Let's Play a Video Game

by Brenda Stein Dzaldov and Cheryl Urback

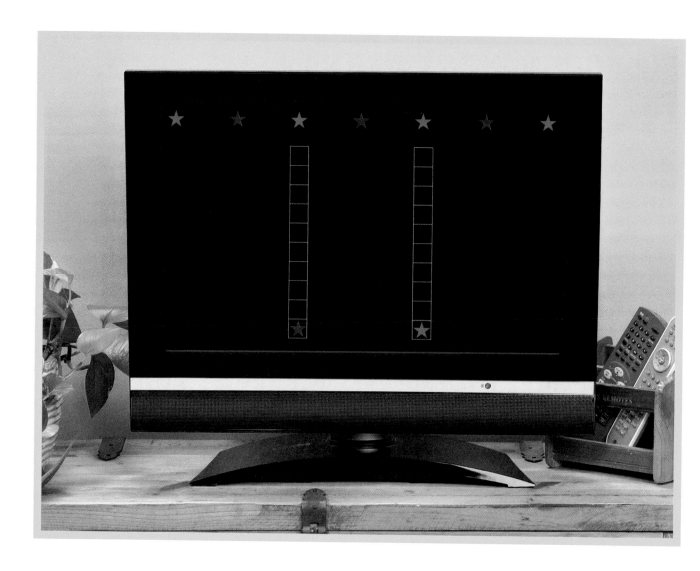

Let's play a video game.

13

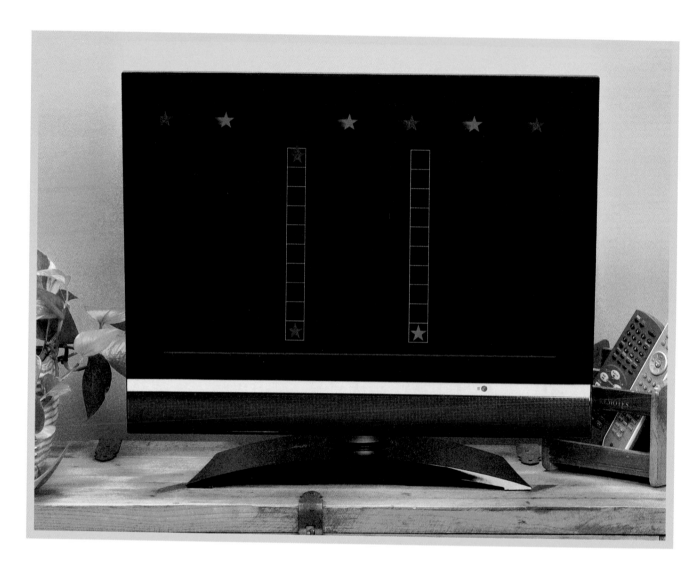

I red star is falling.
Beep!

14

I have more stars.

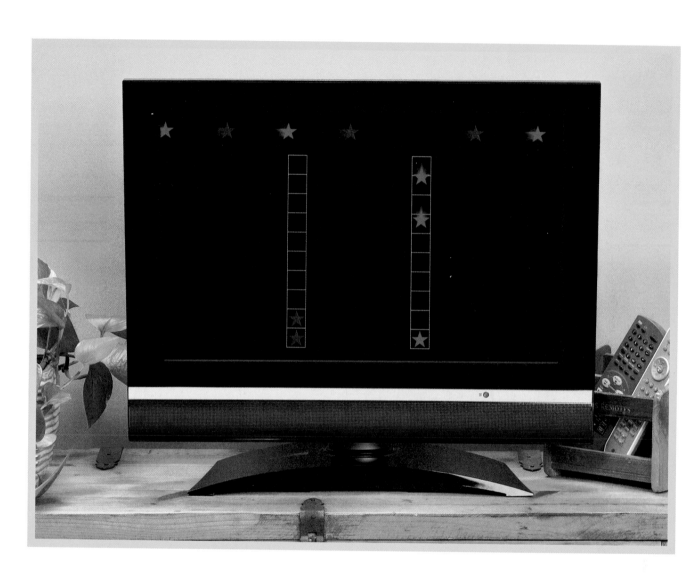

2 blue stars are falling.
Beep! Beep!

I have more stars.

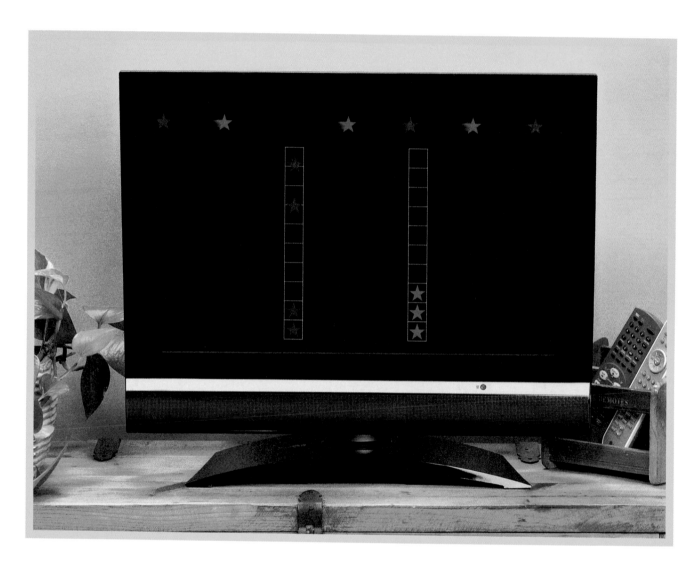

2 red stars are falling.
Beep! Beep!

I have more stars.

19

3 blue stars are falling.
Beep! Beep! Beep!

20

I have more stars.

21

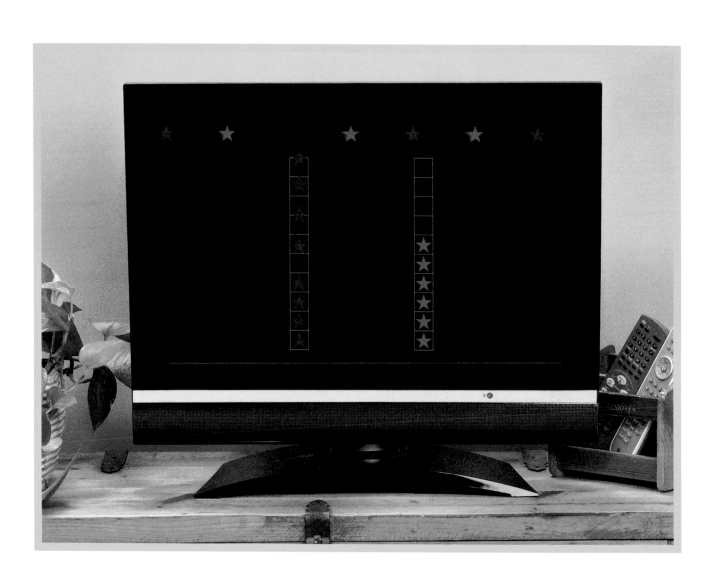

4 red stars are falling.
Beep! Beep! Beep! Beep!

I have more stars.

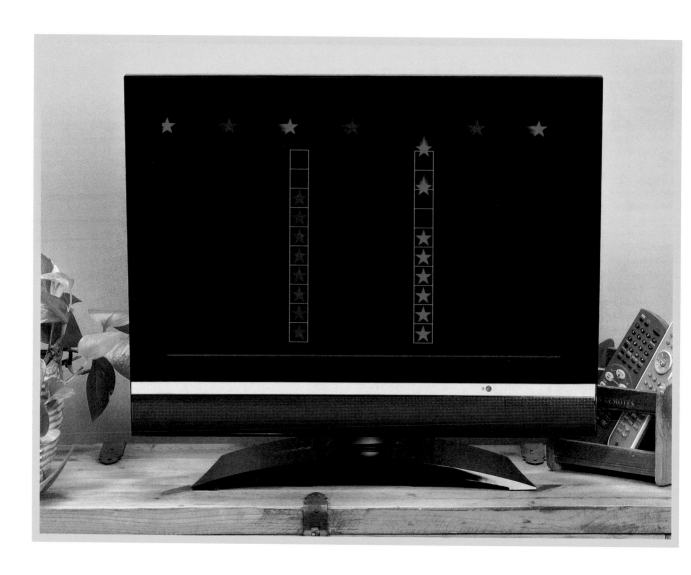

2 blue stars are falling.
Beep! Beep!

I red star is falling.
Beep!

26

I have more stars.

27

2 blue stars are falling.
Beep! Beep!

I win!

Make a Model

Are there more blue stars or more red stars?

Magpies in the Storm

by Jill Bever and Sheilah Currie

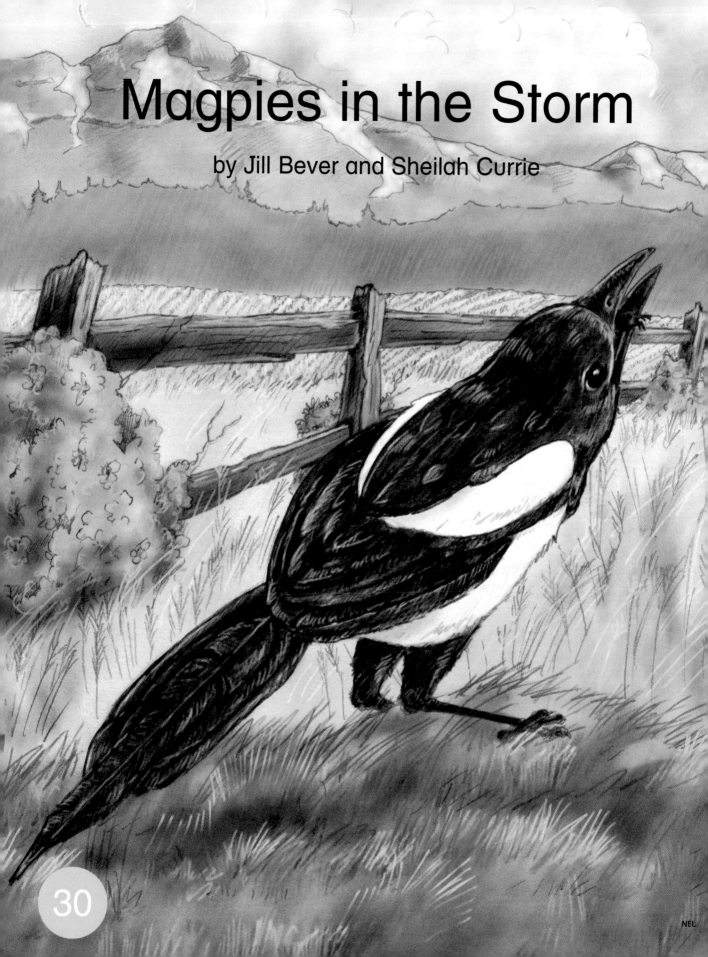

2 magpies are eating bugs.

NEL

6 magpies are eating bugs.

NEL

34

35

NEL

2 magpies are eating bugs.

NEL

Draw a Picture

2 magpies are on the buffalo.
5 more magpies come.
2 fly away.
How many magpies are left?

Look at the Picture

Totem Poles

Draw a log on a strip of paper.
Make it taller than totem pole 1.
Make it shorter than totem pole 2.

Which is longer around: a glass
or a mug?

43

Which container in the kitchen holds the least?

Choice

Which container in the kitchen holds the most?

45

Look at the Picture

The Zoo Train

Tell number stories
about the zoo train.

Make a Model

To Solve the Problem

48

Are there more

or more  ?

How do you know?

Show another way to count the pencils.

Choice

Show another way to count the flowers.

Look at the Picture

At the

Bakery

Tell addition and subtraction
stories for this picture.

Act It Out

8 = 6 + 2

54

Put 6 blue cubes and 2 red cubes on one side.
Put 2 colours of cubes on the other side.
Make the sides balance.

Show different ways.

Josh will use more markers.
Amir will use fewer.
How many more might Josh use?

Choice

Sara has 3 more animals than Dena.
All the animals are on the shelf.
How many does each girl have?

Looking for Shapes at the Mall

by Christine Finochio

Emma went to the mall with her mom.

"Look!" said Emma. "I see a square on the floor."

"Look at the sign," said Emma.
"It is a rectangle."

Mom asked, "Now what shape do you see?"

"I see a triangle," said Emma.

"Look, Mom! Here is a circle,"
said Emma.

Then Emma pointed to the sign
on the door.

"Do you know what this shape is,
Mom?" she asked.

"Yes," said Mom. "It is a square."

"Look," said Emma. "This shape is a rectangle."

"Yes, it is," said Mom.

Emma looked up. "Now I see a triangle," she said.

"Look!" said Mom.
"It's time to go home."

Make a Model

Emma saw these shapes at the mall:

Put together the shapes to make one of these new shapes.

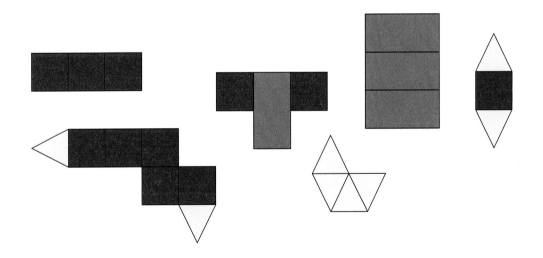

Then use the same shapes to make a different shape. Tell about your shapes.

Look at the Picture

Festival du Voyageur

SNOW SCULPTURES

Tell a 10 + story
about some children
at the festival.

Guess and Test

Riley puts seeds in the feeder.
10 squirrels come to eat.
Some are red and some are grey.
More of the squirrels are red.

What could the number story be?

You have 18¢.
Choose one thing to buy.
How many pennies will you have left?

GARAGE SALE

5 ¢

8 ¢

9 ¢

6 ¢

4 ¢

2 ¢

7 ¢

3 ¢

Choice

Beth is at the garage sale.
She has more than 15 pennies.
She has fewer than 20 pennies.
How many could be in each hand?

Spilled Paint

1	2	3	4	5
11	12	13	14	15
21	22	23	24	25
31	32	33	34	35
		43	44	45
			54	55
61	62	63	64	65
71	72	73	74	75
81	82	83	84	85
91	92	93	94	95

Paint has spilled on the 100 chart.

74

6	7	8	9	10
16	17	18	19	20
26	27	28	29	30
36	37	38	39	40
46	47	48	49	50
56	57	58	59	60
66	67			70
76	77			80
86	87	88	89	90
96	97	98	99	100

Which numbers are missing?

Act It Out

To Solve the Problem

Find the rock that hides the treasure.

1. The rock's number comes before 89.

2. Its number comes after 72.

3. Its number comes between 76 and 84.

4. You say its number when you count by 10s.

NEL

Julie counted backward. She said 7 numbers before these ones. Where did she start?

... 21, 20, 19.

How many numbers did Leo say between 54 and 39?

56, 55, 54, ... 39, 38.

What Will We Make?

by Jill Bever and Sheilah Currie

80

I covered part of this square
with stickers.

I covered this big circle
with loonies.

My circle is the same size.

I covered it with lids.

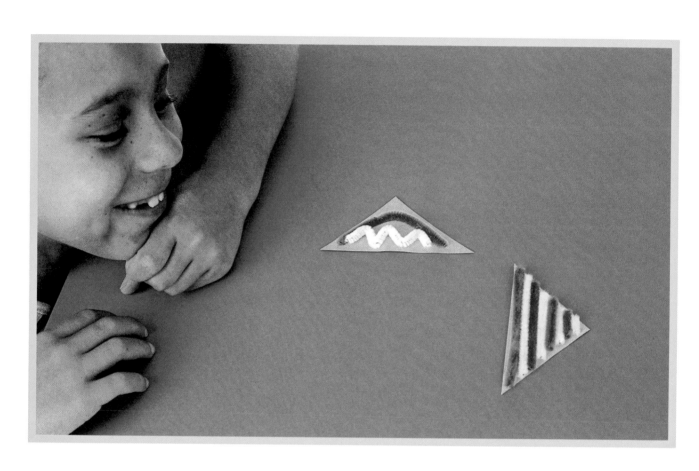

I covered 2 triangles
that are the same size.

I covered 2 more triangles
that are the same size.

This is a small circle.

I covered it with big jellybeans.

This is a small circle, too.

I covered it with small jellybeans.

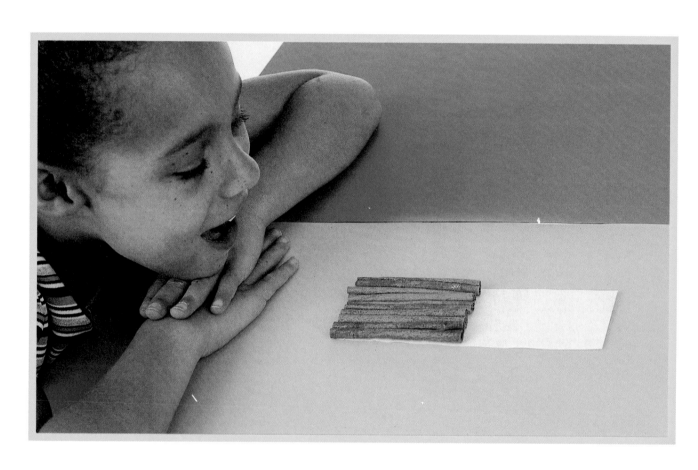

I covered part of this rectangle.

This rectangle is the same size.
I covered all of it.

Here are 4 small triangles.

I covered all of them.

My triangles are the same size.
I covered all of them, too.

We used all of the shapes.
We made a park!

Make a Model

How can you make shapes that are the same size?

Credits